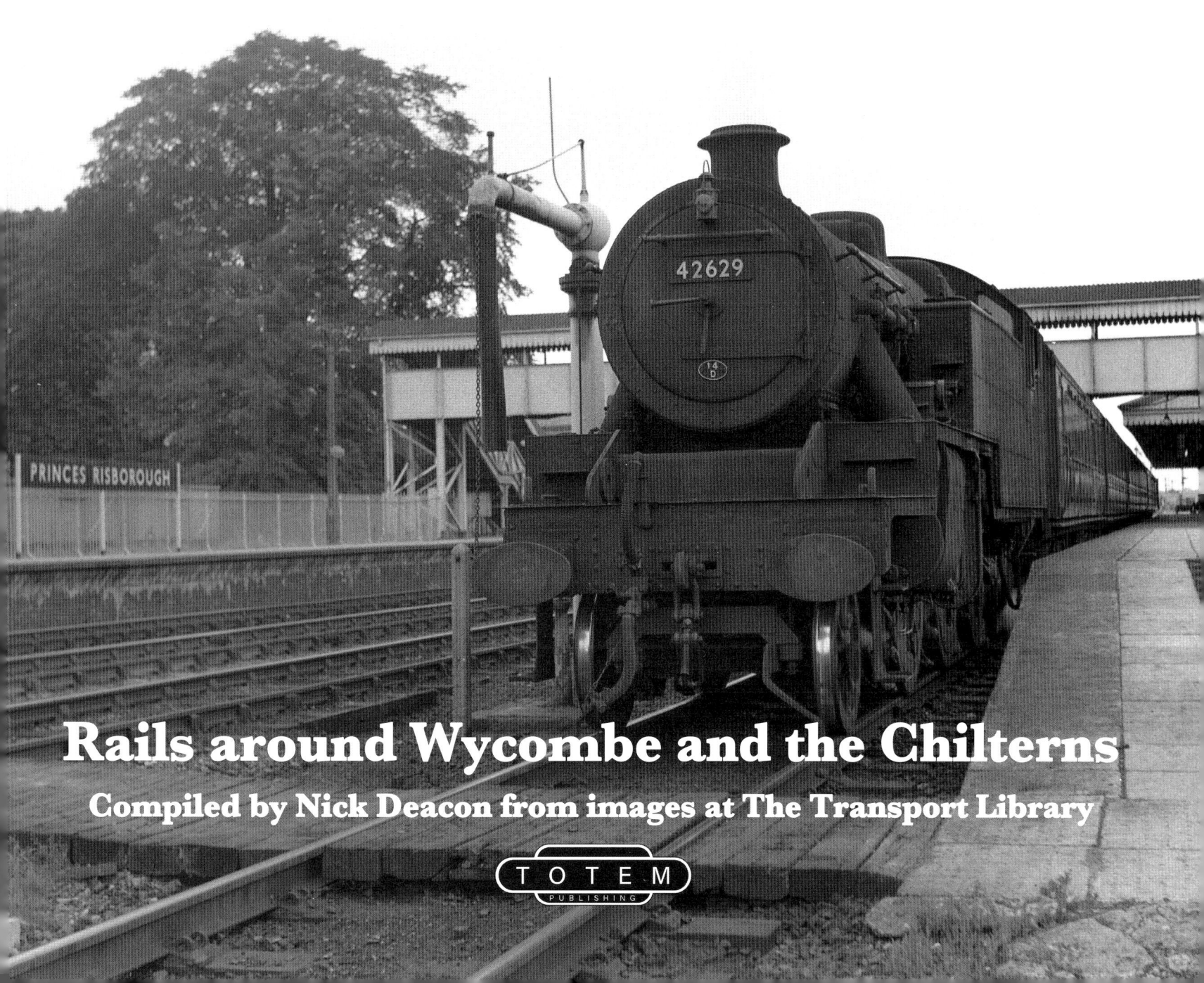

Rails around Wycombe and the Chilterns

Compiled by Nick Deacon from images at The Transport Library

TOTEM
PUBLISHING

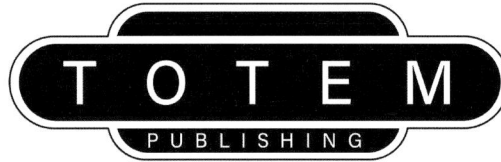

© Images and design:The Transport Treasury 2021.Text: Nick Deacon

ISBN 978-1-913893-09-5

First Published in 2022 by Transport Treasury Publishing Ltd. 16 Highworth Close, High Wycombe, HP13 7PJ

Totem Publishing, an imprint of Transport Treasury Publishing.

www.ttpublishing.co.uk

Printed in Tarxien, Malta by Gutenberg Press Ltd.

'Rails around Wycombe and the Chilterns' is one of a series of books on specialist transport subjects published in strictly limited numbers and produced under the Totem Publishing imprint using material only available at The Transport Treasury.

Front Cover Ref 1. On 7 July 1962, No. 6012 King Edward VI of Stafford Road shed eases a Birkenhead service through the series of reverse curves at High Wycombe which dictated a maximum speed of 35mph. The train is seen to the west of the station having passed under the acutely angled Amersham Hill road bridge and with the huge brick retaining wall serving as an unmistakeable backdrop. 6012, a recent transferee from Old Oak Common, had acquired a double chimney in February 1958, but only had a little over two months left before withdrawal occurred in September after amassing almost two million miles. *M20-6*

Rear cover Ref 2. Taken from the footbridge at Bourne End station on 17 September 1958, this view looks north-east across the Station Road level crossing towards Wooburn Green. An immaculate 61XX 2-6-2T No. 6115 of Slough shed waits for clearance with a service for High Wycombe whilst beyond the interesting bracket signal and crossing gates another Prairie, Oxford's 5190, is similarly held with a southbound freight. After closure of the High Wycombe section in May 1970, the route beyond the level crossing was abandoned making the station a terminus with the line finishing at buffer stops just short of the crossing gates where No. 6115 is standing. The route of the line beyond the gates is now part of the Boston Drive housing development. *H377*

Frontispiece Ref 3. Stanier taper-boiler 2-cylinder 2-6-4T No. 42629 prepares to leave Princes Risborough on 17 August 1960 with the 7.19pm passenger service to Marylebone. At this date, the engine was one of thirty-six of the LMS Fairburn/Stanier 4P mixed traffic types based at Neasden shed for use on the Wycombe/Risborough/Aylesbury suburban traffic as well as similar services over the Met/GCR line. These engines first appeared at the shed from 1954/5 and gradually displaced ex-GCR and LNER types on the services – particularly after the transfer of the shed from Eastern Region to London Midland Region control in February 1958 when the shed code was changed from 34E to 14D. *H1727*

Introduction

The small towns, villages and hamlets scattered throughout the Chiltern woodlands and their rich agricultural apron of the Vale of Aylesbury were traditionally known as 'the larder of London' long before the coming of the railway. The topology of the region is dominated by the band of chalk hills running in a general south-west to north-east direction from the Thames Valley to Hertfordshire and passage through them was determined by the presence of natural gaps through which roads and railways could be funnelled. However, after the GWR and L&NWR had forged their respective trunk routes out from London and with the latter opening their branch from Cheddington to Aylesbury in 1839, a decade or more would pass until the untapped area between the two heavyweights was harnessed into the railway network.

The first scheme to be launched was promoted by the Wycombe Railway and given Parliamentary assent in 1846, but it was not until 1854 after a protracted lease and working arrangement was concluded with the GWR that a broad gauge line from Maidenhead via Bourne End (or 'Marlow Road' as it was named for the first few years) reached High Wycombe. From then on matters accelerated with a complex flurry of Bills promoting extensions to the Wycombe Railway, these being to Thame via Princes Risborough opened in August 1862, to Aylesbury from Princes Risborough opened in October 1863 and to Oxford from Thame opened in October 1864. All these lines were laid to broad gauge, leased to the GWR and worked by them from the beginning, and so it was no surprise when, in January 1867, the GWR absorbed the Wycombe Railway and took on its considerable outstanding debts.

As early as 1868, plans were drawn up to convert all of these broad gauge lines to standard gauge and a start was made with the Aylesbury branch later that year with the remainder converted by August 1870. The Watlington & Princes Risborough Railway (W&PRR) was the next addition to the railway scene when it opened as a standard gauge branch in August 1872. However, the concern only lasted as a debt-ridden independent company until 1883 when it was liquidated and then purchased by the GWR for a knock-down price of £23,000 in the same year – almost half of what it had cost to build.

Lastly, hard on the heels of the W&PRR, came The Great Marlow Railway which opened through to Marlow Road (later renamed 'Bourne End') on 27 June 1873. This company, although operated with GWR stock and underpinned with a supportive level of their investment, managed to remain an independent concern until amalgamated with the GWR as from 1 July 1897. Although the completion of all these initiatives had brought South Buckinghamshire quite a substantial railway network, access to London from Aylesbury, High Wycombe, Princes Risborough or Thame remained only what could be best described as 'circuitous', requiring travel to Maidenhead or Oxford.

This situation was dramatically solved by a collaboration between the GCR and GWR which resulted in the passage of the August 1899 Bill forming the Great Western & Great Central Joint Committee. The strategic remit of the joint concern was to provide firstly, the GWR a more direct Birmingham – London link and secondly, the GCR an alternative route into their new London terminus at Marylebone. The ambitious project involved the construction of new sections between Northolt and High Wycombe, the purchase and upgrading of the existing High Wycombe – Princes Risborough section and the construction of another new section from Princes Risborough to the GCR main line at Grendon Underwood. The joint venture was opened throughout for goods traffic in November 1905 and for passengers from 2 April 1906. For the GWR, the icing on the cake came with the opening in 1910 of the so-called 'Bicester Cut-Off' which created a new link of their ownership from a new junction north of Princes Risborough where the GCR branched off (Ashendon Jct.) onwards to a point just south of Banbury on the Oxford line (Aynho Jct.).

For High Wycombe in particular the new route (and the new station it brought to the town) transformed its fortunes from being merely a feeder on a local branch line to that of occupying an important location on a major though route. To a lesser extent, Princes Risborough also benefitted alongside its role as a focal point for the three other lines coming in from Aylesbury, Oxford/Thame and Watlington.

The purpose of this book is to convey something illustrative of the diverse flavour of the 1950s and '60s steam railway which could be found on these lines before the dragnet of 'modern improvements' and closures irrevocably changed such scenes. Starting at Gerrards Cross and moving northwards, the photographic journey fans out from High Wycombe to Maidenhead and Marlow, continues northwards along the main line to Princes Risborough, along the Aylesbury and Watlington branches plus the Oxford branch as far as Thame, and a little further along the main line as far as Haddenham.

Sources consulted:
The Oxford to Princes Risborough – A GWR Secondary Route. C.R. Potts. Oakwood Press 2004.
The GWR & GCR Joint Railway. Stanley C. Jenkins. Oakwood Press 2006.
The Marlow Branch. Paul Karau & Chris Turner. Wild Swan Pubs. Ltd. 1987.
Country Branch Line. Vols 1 & 2. Paul Karau & Chris Turner. Wild Swan Pubs. Ltd. 1998.
GWR Engine Sheds London Division. Chris Hawkins & George Reeve. Wild Swan Pubs. Ltd. 1987.
GWR Journal – various issues. Wild Swan Pubs. Ltd.
British Railway Journal – various issues. Wild Swan Pubs. Ltd.

Sketch Map of the Railways Covered by the Book
Created by Nick Deacon

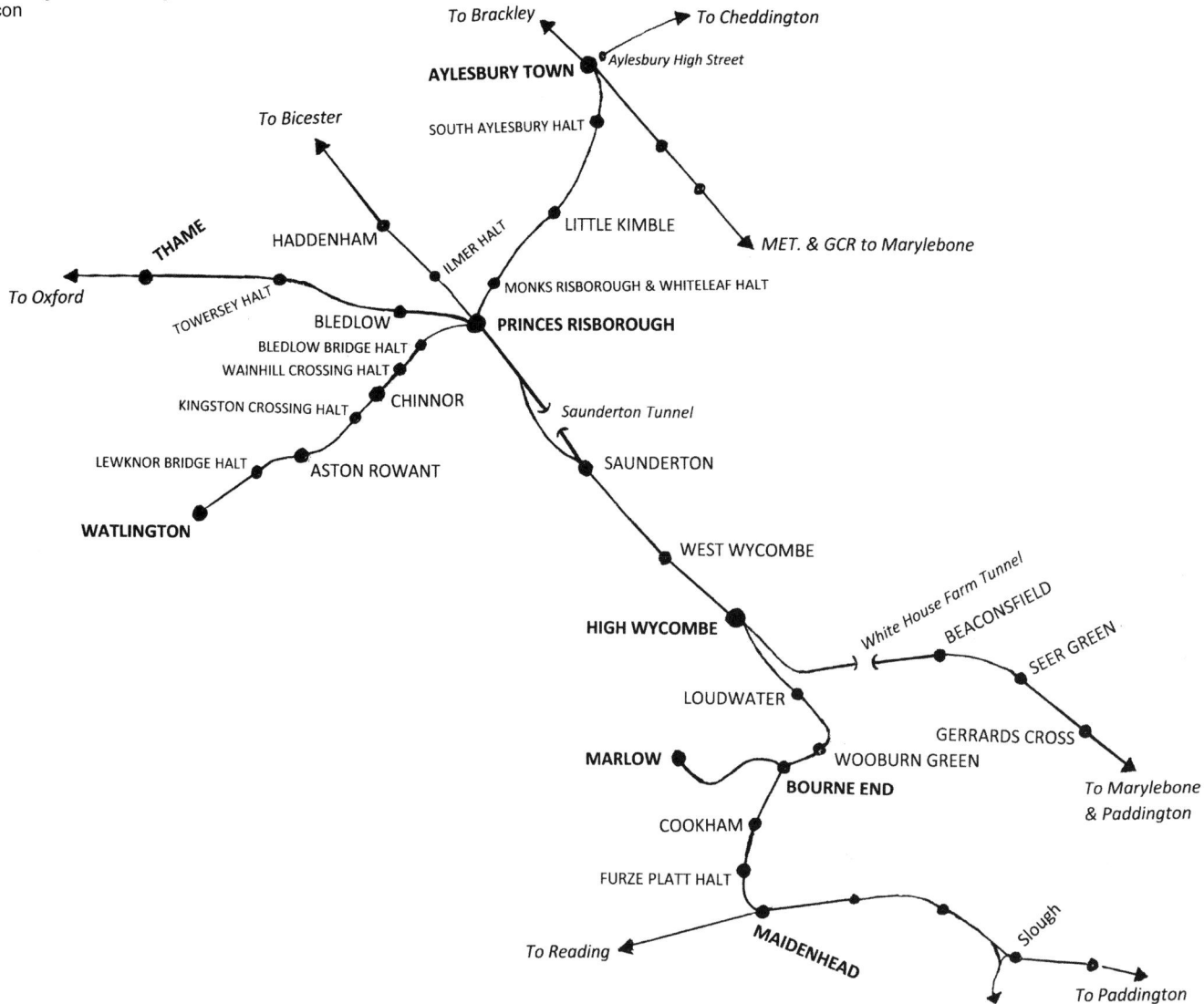

To Brackley

To Cheddington

AYLESBURY TOWN — Aylesbury High Street

To Bicester

SOUTH AYLESBURY HALT

THAME

HADDENHAM

ILMER HALT

LITTLE KIMBLE

MET. & GCR to Marylebone

To Oxford

TOWERSEY HALT

BLEDLOW

MONKS RISBOROUGH & WHITELEAF HALT

PRINCES RISBOROUGH

BLEDLOW BRIDGE HALT

WAINHILL CROSSING HALT

KINGSTON CROSSING HALT

CHINNOR

Saunderton Tunnel

LEWKNOR BRIDGE HALT

ASTON ROWANT

SAUNDERTON

WATLINGTON

WEST WYCOMBE

HIGH WYCOMBE

White House Farm Tunnel

BEACONSFIELD

SEER GREEN

LOUDWATER

MARLOW

WOOBURN GREEN

GERRARDS CROSS

BOURNE END

To Marylebone & Paddington

COOKHAM

FURZE PLATT HALT

MAIDENHEAD

Slough

To Reading

To Paddington

4

Ref 4. The generous track layout at Gerrards Cross was typical of the new passenger stations opened along the route of the GWR/GCR Joint Railway from 2 April 1906. It is seen to good effect here with 'Black 5' No. 45217 of Annesley shed running effortlessly through with the Up 1X55 Saturday special from Sutton-in-Ashfield, Mansfield, on 27 April 1963 – one of five such specials from the Midlands area recorded by the photographer that day; probably booked in conjunction with the Schoolboy Football International between England and Wales. A gate of 90,000 watched England win 4-1. *AS N40-5*

Ref 5. On 10 June 1961, No. 6853 Morehampton Grange of Tyseley shed passes under the Packhorse Road bridge and enters the lengthy Down platform loop of Gerrards Cross station with assorted carriage stock forming a troop special. In order to minimise gradient challenges at this location the station area was built in a cutting which required the removal of 1,300,000 cubic yards of earth. The engine was new to Tyseley in November 1937 and remained there for the duration of her career until withdrawal during October 1965. She was scrapped at the G. Cohen yard at Kettering.
Nicolson 5-65-2

Ref 6. In the early 1960s No. 5022 Wigmore Castle waits to depart from Gerrards Cross with the northbound H48 Birmingham stopper service from Paddington. 5022 received a double chimney early in 1959 and from 1948 until her withdrawal in June 1963 was based at Wolverhampton Stafford Road shed. The engine was new to traffic in August 1932 and spent the first fourteen years of her career at Old Oak Common and was named after a ruined 11th Century castle located on the Welsh Marches in north-west Herefordshire.
Potton 457-3

Ref 7. The photographer Dick Riley had the privilege of recording many footplate rides over the years and this was one of them with 6003 King George IV on 23 April 1960. The engine had just returned to Old Oak Common after receiving its very last Heavy General overhaul at Swindon between December '59 and March '60 and was in tip-top condition. Dick photographed the way ahead as the train had passed north through Gerrards Cross and was heading towards the Bull Lane road bridge. The siding on the right containing the ballast train ran back towards Gerrards Cross station. Five months later No. 6003, along with other classmates, was transferred to Cardiff Canton shed but due to the lack of appropriate work available to her type and weight, spent much time in store. She returned to Old Oak in February '62 and was withdrawn from there on 25 June 1962. *RCR14675*

Ref 8. Heading north towards Seer Green & Jordans station in the summer of 1957, ex-GCR Robinson Class A5 4-6-2T No. 69828 passes under the Potkin Lane road bridge as it makes a rare return visit to its old haunts for which it was built for in 1923 – working the GCR Marylebone suburban services. However, by 1954 the class (including 69828) had been displaced from Neasden shed by LNER Thompson L1 2-6-4Ts - an unpopular move with some footplate crews who preferred the Robinson engines. 69828 finished its career at Colwick shed, Nottingham, where she was withdrawn in November 1958. *Stead NS202677*

Ref 9. A verdant summer scene in the cutting west of Beaconsfield sometime in the early 1960s. WD 2-8-0 No. 90188 drifts south with a lengthy Class H mineral train for London – possibly originating from the South Yorkshire coalfield as the engine was based around this time at Mexborough shed near Rotherham. She was withdrawn from Barrow Hill shed, Bristol, in April 1965 and broken up by that great devourer of steam engines, Cashmore's of Great Bridge, Tipton. Although reliable performers even in advanced states of dishevelment, GWR drivers were never keen on the type regarding them as 'sullen' performers, preferring their home-grown 28XX and 38XX 2-8-0s on these kinds of freight duties.
Potton 455-6

Ref 10. Seen in the same cutting as the WD and probably photographed on the same day, Collett 4-6-0 No. 4950 Patshull Hall heads north to the west of Beaconsfield with a Class H through freight. For most of the 1950s the engine was based at Laira and Penzance sheds before migrating 'up country' in October 1960 to Didcot where she finished her career in May 1964 after completing over 1.3m miles in service. The engine was named after the Grade 1 listed Georgian mansion house built in 1730 and located near Pattingham in Staffordshire.
Potton 455-5

Ref 11. High Wycombe South signal box was situated on the Down side of the line a short distance to the west of the junction with the Maidenhead line. It was the largest of the three 'boxes in the immediate area; the others being 'Middle' and 'North'. 'South' was a GWR 93-lever 5 bar V tappet type which opened in 1905 ready for the completion of the Joint GWR/GCR through route for goods in November of the same year and for passengers in April 1906. Rationalisation of the signalling arrangements resulted in the closure of the 'box in late February/early March 1991. A notable feature in this photograph is the elevated positioning of a ground disc signal on the platform of a modified semaphore post for sighting purposes – an unusual but not completely unknown adaptation. *JGS002919*

Ref 12. Although a similar shot is featured on the front cover of this book, it is impossible to resist another visit to the west of High Wycombe and its huge retaining wall with a chance to dwell on the sight of another 'King' on a Down Paddington express. This shot was taken on 4 April 1958 and features immaculate No. 6022 King Edward III of Old Oak Common shed with the 11.10am Wolverhampton service. It has to be said that the engine's appearance is enhanced by the absence of the disfiguring train reporting number and frame usually affixed to the front of the smokebox! No. 6022 benefitted from new front frames and inside cylinders in November 1954 and received a double chimney in May 1956. It moved to Stafford Road shed in June 1959 and remained there until September 1962 when it was condemned. *RCR11537*

Ref 13. Tucked away in the Down platform bay at High Wycombe on 3 March 1957 is Collett 0-4-2T No. 1448 and its single autotrailer on the Maidenhead branch duty. The engine was completed in April 1935 and became a long-term resident at Slough shed, becoming a regular performer on the branch until its withdrawal in June 1960. The autotrailer looks to be one of the GWR Diagram L 1906/7 vehicles with American bogies – a type known to have worked on the branch until the late 1950s.
LN671

Ref 14. The staggered nature of the High Wycombe platforms is evident in this shot of No. 6014 *King Henry VII* passing through on 4 March 1961 with the 2.10pm M18 service from Paddington to Birkenhead. The engine has the wedge-shaped cab fitted as part of the 1935 streamlining exercise and received a double chimney in September 1957. During a works visit in early 1954, No. 6014 was also fitted with a new type of blow-down apparatus and a device in the cab which collected boiler water samples to check the deposit formations. This was developed in conjunction with ICI and after fitting the engine was permanently transferred to Stafford Road shed to be nearer Wolverhampton-based ICI specialists to monitor the equipment and analyse its results. Along with thirteen of her classmates, No. 6014 was withdrawn in September 1962. *H2038*

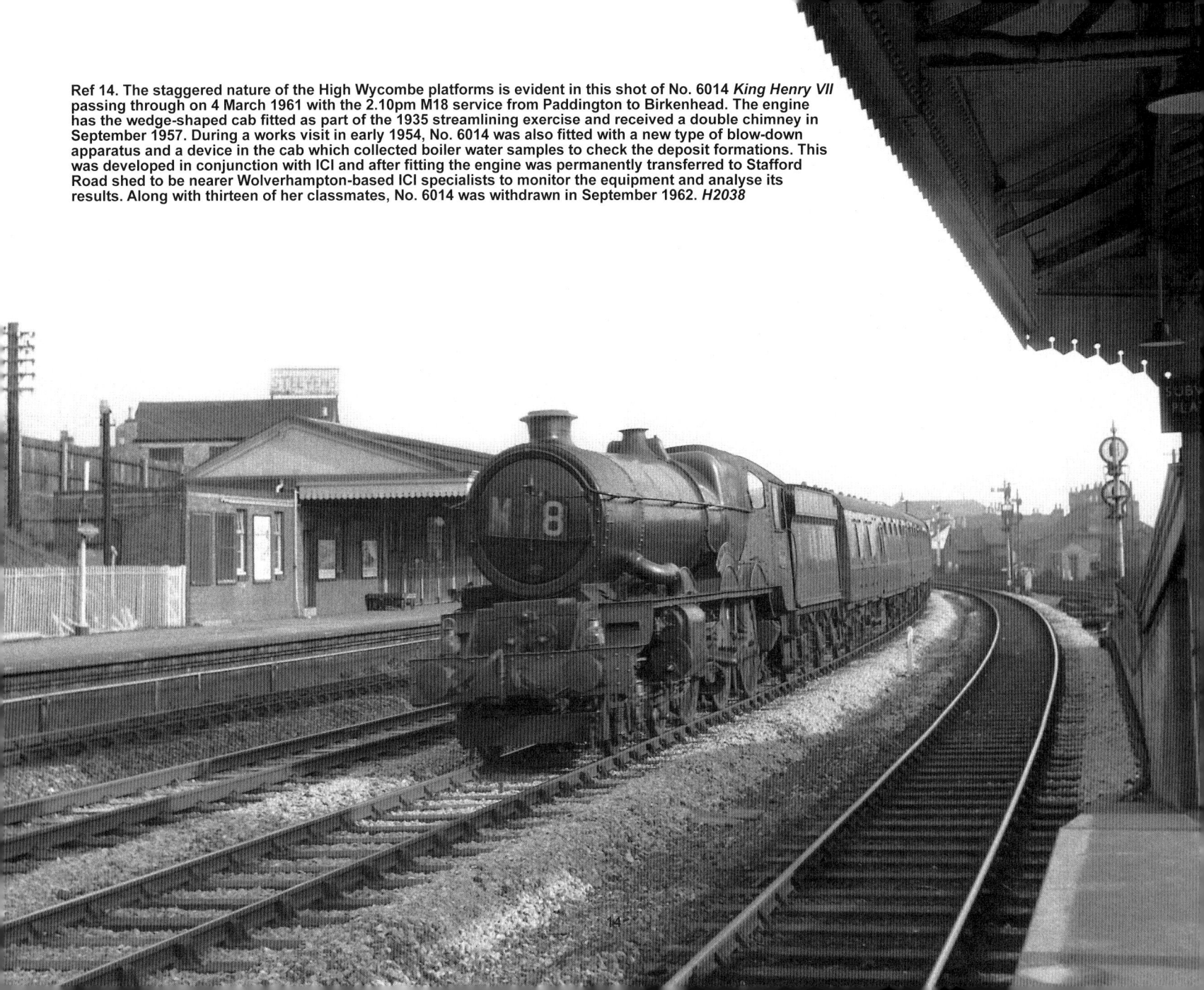

Ref 15. On 4 March 1961 LMS Class 4MT Fairburn 2-6-4T No. 42251 approaches the Up platform at High Wycombe with the empty carriage stock forming the 3.10pm departure for Marylebone. The engine was one of a number of the type transferred in 1954/5 from the London, Tilbury & Southend section to Neasden shed to gradually replace the LNER Thompson L1 2-6-4T engines - a process which had been completed by 1959 when 27 of the LMS class were on Neasden's books. No. 42251 remained on the Marylebone services until June 1962 when it was moved to Woodford Halse shed followed by a succession of moves which took the engine further north until it finished its career at Low Moor shed, Bradford, in October 1967. *H2041*

Ref 16. This view taken on 4 April 1958 looks north from the Amersham Hill road bridge towards the footbridge connecting Castle Street and Priory Avenue. Just beyond the latter on the Down side of the line 'Middle' signal box is visible. Thompson Class L1 2-6-4T No. 67747 approaches with stock for a Marylebone stopping service. The newly built class first appeared at Neasden shed in February 1948 and others followed until over one third of the class of 100 were allocated there for the Marylebone suburban services as replacements for the aging GCR Robinson A5 4-6-2Ts. No. 67747 remained at Neasden until June 1958 when it moved briefly to Willesden and then gravitated further north to finally succumb in July 1962 from Colwick shed, Nottingham – the year which saw the elimination of the class.
RCR 11538

Left Top, Ref 17. Although most Saturday Only South Coast services to locations such as Margate or Ramsgate from the Midlands and the North were routed via Banbury-Oxford-Reading, there were a few exceptions run along the Joint line and the West London route via Kensington Olympia. One example of a returning service is seen on 7 July 1962 west of High Wycombe hauled by Sheffield Darnall-based Class B1 4-6-0 No. 61181 which the photographer recorded as having originated from Nottinghamshire. The B1 would have come off the southbound train at Kensington Olympia, run to Old Oak Common for servicing before returning to Kensington to collect the northbound service. The summer of 1962 was particularly busy on the Birmingham route as additional trains were run to compensate for a reduced service on the West Coast Main Line from Euston caused by the ongoing electrification works.
AS M20-5

Left Bottom, Ref 18. On 23 March 1957 Slough-based 57XX 0-6-0PT No. 4680 pauses between duties on the High Wycombe Down through line. Apart from through goods traffic, High Wycombe generated business from its two yards; North, situated to the west of the station on the Down side of the line, South, alongside the station plus two private sidings including one to the south of the station for E. Gomme Ltd, the famous furniture manufacturer. No. 4680 and its happy driver may possibly be on local pilot or trip duties between the two yards having come up from Maidenhead on a local freight. The engine survived until the last of GWR steam and was not withdrawn until early January 1966 from Worcester shed.
LRF2699

Right, Ref 19. On 23 March 1957, an immaculate Thompson Class L1 No. 67740 prepares to leave High Wycombe with the 12.30pm service to Marylebone. The engine was a regular on these suburban duties at the time and is a credit to Neasden shed which often struggled with staff shortages in the BR era. The engine first arrived in August 1953 from Stratford and remained until June 1958 when it was transferred briefly to Willesden shed. It spent the final three years of its short 12 year 8 month life at the ex-Great Central shed at Woodford Halse where it was withdrawn in July 1961.
LRF2700

Ref 20. On 7 July 1962 No. 6015 *King Richard III* of Stafford Road shed drifts past High Wycombe North signal box with an Up service. The reporting number 'B10' appears to have been unchanged from a previous Bristol duty as Up Joint line expresses were either 'Axx' if from Wolverhampton, Birmingham or Shrewsbury or 'Vxx' from Birkenhead. The engine was the first of the class to receive a double chimney in September 1955 and shortly after this, while working the 'Cornish Riviera' express, attained a speed of over 107mph – the highest authenticated speed ever achieved by a GWR engine. By this date of the photo, the class had entered their last operational summer and No. 6015, recently transferred from Old Oak Common, survived for just a few weeks longer. At the end of July, it was reported as being out of use at Stafford Road shed and was officially withdrawn during September.
AS M21

Ref 21. Maidenhead, on the GWR main line, became a junction from 1 August 1854 with the arrival of the Wycombe Railway. The junction lay 1½ miles west of the first 'Maidenhead & Taplow' station which was replaced in 1871/2 by the present station located close to the junction. The new station was provided with two main line platforms, a bay and a train shed for the Wycombe services on the north side. The station was enlarged in 1891 for the quadrupling of the main line. Slough shed's 61XX No. 6160 was a regular performer on the branch at this time and is waiting to leave Maidenhead's platform 5 with the 1.51pm service for High Wycombe on 17 September 1958. *JH366*

Ref 22. Through services from Paddington to High Wycombe via Maidenhead continued during the early 1960s, but in the last years up to the closure of the northern section of the branch this was reduced to a shuttle service between Bourne End-High Wycombe. Another of Slough shed's stable of 61XXs, this time No. 6117, takes water at the west end of Maidenhead's Down relief platform with the 1pm service from Paddington on 4 March 1961. The connection to the branch can be seen curving away to the right. *JH2036*

Ref 23. Furze Platt Halt is 1 mile 22 chains from Maidenhead station and was opened by the GWR on 5 July 1937 as a response to the growth of population in the North Town and Furze Platt areas of Maidenhead. The halt was accessed from the level crossing at Harrow Lane and consisted of a simple boarded platform on the west side of the line equipped with a wooden shelter. Collett 14XX 0-4-2T No. 1445 calls with a northbound autotrailer service sometime in the early 1960s. Helping to date the photograph it is known that the engine was based at Slough shed between October 1961 and December 1963 when it moved to Gloucester. The station remains open for business, but the boarded platform and wooden shelter have long since been replaced. *LS726*

Ref 24. The attractive Cookham station photographed on 22 May 1961 with a 14XX engine with an Up autotrailer service from High Wycombe. At 2 miles 73 chains 'out' from Maidenhead, the station is situated south of the level crossing at the bottom of Station Hill. Opened on 1 August 1854, the brick and flint-built station was provided with a passing loop, two platforms, a connecting footbridge and a Type 5 GWR 21-lever signal box. The station is still open but has now been reduced to a single line and platform. Fortunately, the station building also survives. *PY10006C*

Ref 25. Cookham station as seen from a passing train on 17 September 1958, featuring the brick and flint 2-storey station building on the Up platform with an attached single storey wing containing the other station facilities. *H367*

Ref 26. At 4 miles 33 chains from Maidenhead and symbolising the essence of a country junction station, a well-groomed Bourne End station basks in early spring sunshine on 4 March 1961. The view looks north towards Station Road level crossing with, from right to left, the goods shed, the Up or Maidenhead platform and waiting room, the Down or Wycombe platform with the main station buildings and the single line bay for the Marlow services which at an earlier date also contained an engine run-round loop. Of particular note is the attractive combination of platform post lighting; that nearest on the right being of a standard GWR design and with the later addition a taller swan-necked type which is also seen at track level on the left. *H2024*

Ref 27. On 23 March 1957, Hawksworth 94XX 0-6-0PT No. 9424 heads the Down 10.12am Maidenhead to High Wycombe service at Bourne End. When new in August 1950, the engine was sent to Slough shed and a year later was joined by classmate No. 9406. Both engines were regular performers on the branch and as High Wycombe was an out-station of Slough shed, both were also used on pilot engine duties there. No.9424 remained at Slough until reallocated to Ebbw Junction shed in September 1960 where she was withdrawn in November 1962.
LRF2688

Ref 28. A portrait of 14XX No. 1421 with autotrailer No. W229W looking south from the Down platform of Bourne End on 4 March 1961 with a service from High Wycombe to Marlow which is already 'pegged' to leave. The engine was based at Reading shed and may be filling in for one of the three regular Slough performers at this date (Nos. 1447/53 & 74) which had been away on a works visit. The engine was moved to Exeter in November 1962 for one year before finishing her days at Gloucester Barnwood shed in December 1963. W229W was a Diagram A38 63ft vehicle built in June 1951 and lasting until late 1960. *H2017*

Ref 29. On 1 July 1962 – just six days before steam finished on the Marlow branch – No. 1445 of Slough shed pulls into Bourne End with the 4.18pm service from Marlow. The photograph was taken from the gallery of the bracket signal on the Down platform and shows the 1956 remodelled junction layout – a project which also included the closure and removal of the South signal box which was sited to the left of the surviving lamp hut in the 'V' of the Marlow branch and the three sidings to the left. No. 1445 hung on at Slough until December 1963 when she was transferred to Gloucester as a replacement for classmate No. 1421 and was withdrawn from Barnwood shed in September 1964. *LS716*

Ref 30. On 7 July 1962 (the last day of steam on the Marlow branch) Slough shed's respectably clean 61XX No. 6128 passes the Bourne End North signal box and level crossing and enters the station with a southbound Class J freight from High Wycombe. There were several freight duties each way between Oxford, Taplow and Slough which required work at High Wycombe, and it is likely this was one of them. No. 6128 finally left Slough in May 1964 and finished at Gloucester Horton Road shed in March 1965. The North signal box had been structurally extended in 1956 to contain the new 44-lever frame as a result of the layout remodelling and the closure of the South 'box. *LS778*

Ref 31. The exterior of Marlow station and its goods shed seen on 17 September 1958. The 2 mile 58 chain 'Great Marlow Railway' branch from Bourne End was opened for goods from 5 July 1873 and for passengers a week later. The line was largely underwritten with GWR financial support and operated with their rolling stock and from the start was a success. The station building was a handsome GWR-designed structure similar to those already seen at Hungerford and Taplow and survived intact until demolished after freight services were withdrawn in July 1966. A new passenger station of the most basic type was opened on 10 July 1967 on a remodelled site formerly containing the goods yard. *JH369*

Ref 32. At Marlow looking towards the buffer stops on 17 September 1958 with 'The Donkey' service – in this case Collett 14XX No. 1448 of Slough shed providing the 'one engine in steam' operation in use since September 1954 when Marlow signal box was closed. The main station building with the projecting canopy contained the booking office, general waiting room, ladies' waiting room and lavatory whilst the wing in the foreground contained the parcels office, a cloakroom, a staffroom used by train crews and the gentlemens' lavatory. Although appearing to be flat roofed, the brick parapet concealed a low hipped roof. The station remained gas lit from the town supply until its replacement in 1967. *H373*

Ref 33. On 23 March 1957 14XX No. 1450 is seen after arrival at Marlow with the 10.39am service from Maidenhead. At about this time and until the end of steam services, the branch train made four return through trips to Maidenhead and three to High Wycombe and, unlike many similar branches up and down the country, never had to compete with any serious threat from bus services. Annual passenger receipts actually rose from £42,360 to almost £50,500 in 1957 (excluding season tickets) and parcels and other goods income remained steady at respectable levels which compared favourably with pre-war WW2 levels. No. 1450 moved to Oxford in September 1959 and then to the West Country to finish eventually at Exmouth Junction shed in May 1965. *LRF2691.*

Ref 34. The engine shed building at Marlow, seen here on 17 September 1958, probably owed its design to the Great Marlow Railway rather than to the GWR, but was improved and probably extended by the latter in 1892. The gable-ended building was 51ft 6in. long and 17ft 6in. wide and constructed in red brick under a slate roof. Until 1948 it had its own allocation of one or two engines for the branch work and as such regarded as a 'sub' to Slough shed. The shed footplate complement was usually two drivers and three firemen with Slough shed covering all the relief work. *H371*

Ref 35. Coaling the hard way at Marlow on 4 March 1961. No. 1421 is featured once more as two chaps labour over the task. Ideally, it was preferable to coal the bunker directly from a wagon parked up to the rear of the engine to save double movement of the coal from wagon to stage and from stage to bunker, but here it has not been possible. Typically, 'The Donkey' services covered over 200 miles daily with the engine returning once a week to Slough for a boiler washout. *H2015*

Left, Ref 36. Sunday 7 July 1962 was the last day of steam operations on the Marlow branch and in this view Reading shed's 14XX No. 1421 was once more on hand and 'bulled up' for the occasion. The train is approaching Bourne End within the stipulated 10mph limit for the class at this point and, unusually, was photographed from the Bourne End Up branch home bracket signal. The train is passing over Brooksby Crossing (with a small boy somewhat forlornly watching its progress) and, to the rear of the autotrailer, is Marina Crossing which led to the riverside wharf and boatyard. Just visible around the curvature of the line is the beginning of the plate girder bridge which crossed the Abbotsbrook backwater, a tributary of the River Thames. *LS724*

Right Top, Ref 37. An animated scene at Wooburn Green station (5 miles 63 chains from Maidenhead) on 4 March 1961 as the autotrailer service is about to leave the single platform with an Up service to Bourne End and Maidenhead. Like other stations on the line, there was a substantial brick and flint 2-storey station house with a single storey wing plus a platform-mounted signal box. Behind the signal box can be seen a yard crane which was used in the small goods yard which was junctioned off to the south of station. Immediately to the north of the station was a level crossing carrying Whitepit Lane over the line. Also of interest is the token setting down apparatus and catch net seen on the left of the coach. After becoming a pay train halt in 1968, the station closed on 4 May 1970 and the buildings were eventually demolished to make way for a housing development. *H2032*

Right Bottom, Ref 38. The last station on the line before High Wycombe was the picturesquely sited Loudwater (7 miles 20 chains from Maidenhead) which also served the adjacent village of Flackwell Heath. The Maidenhead autotrailer service with W229W awaits departure on 4 March 1961. The station had two platforms and a spacious goods yard with four sidings located on the north side of the line behind the main buildings. Loudwater suffered the same decline in status as Wooburn Green and was also closed at the same date. The station site is now largely under the route of the M40, and the goods yard site is now a small industrial estate. *H2030*

Above, Ref 38A. On 4 March 1961, Large Prairie 2-6-2T No. 6117 of Slough shed has arrived at Loudwater with the Down 1pm departure from Paddington and is 'pegged' to leave for High Wycombe across Station Road level crossing. Seen above the engine is the GWR Type 5 25-lever signal box. No. 6117 remained in the London area and was withdrawn from Southall shed in September 1965. *JH2037*

Right, Ref 39. Passing trains at Loudwater on 23 March 1957. We have already seen Hawksworth 94XX No. 9424 at Bourne End, but it is now seen heading another Maidenhead to High Wycombe service on the same day at Loudwater station. As it enters the Down loop the driver keeps an eye out for unwary heads on a southbound service. The engine spent ten years at Slough shed from August 1950 until September 1960 and was regularly seen on the Wycombe goods and passenger services. *LRF2701*

Ref 40. Class L1 2-6-4T No. 67740, seen previously at High Wycombe, leaves West Wycombe station in its wake as it heads for High Wycombe with an Up stopping service to Marylebone on 28 April 1956. At the time of the photograph Neasden shed had sixteen of the class on its books which were still in regular use on the High Wycombe/Princes Risborough/Aylesbury Joint line services as well as on the GCR main line. The influx of LMS 2-6-4Ts at Neasden mentioned elsewhere was said to have been prompted by the L1s suffering a high incidence of hot boxes and motion problems – a situation exacerbated by severe maintenance staff shortages at the shed which occasionally led to train cancellations. *RCR7161*

Ref 41. The station at West Wycombe had existed since 1862 when the Wycombe Railway had opened its single line extension through to Princes Risborough and Thame on 1 August of that year. The station was remodelled in 1905/6 in conjunction with the opening of the Joint line with the Down side buildings rebuilt, a new Up platform installed with a building and footbridge, and a goods yard located to the east of the station on the Down side of the line. Although laid out for quadruple track, only two were ever laid. The neat assembly of the Up side building is shown to good effect in this early 1950s view including an interesting assortment of GWR and LNER signage reflecting the former 'joint' ownership of the station. Regrettably, the station closed on 3 November 1958 but in recent years has been mooted for a reopening given the westward spread of High Wycombe. *JH39*

Ref 42. On 28 April 1956 No. 6011 *King James I* hurries through West Wycombe with an Up express. The yard on the Down side of the line is shown to good effect although with only one mineral wagon standing just beyond the loading gauge; the activity can only have been minimal despite the presence of a few lorries. On maps dated c.1960 the area, although still rail-served, is described as a 'transport depot' which suggests the emphasis had shifted towards a base for road haulage. No. 6011 was allocated to Stafford Road shed at this time and moved to Old Oak in September 1962 and was believed to be the last normal revenue-earning 'King' in service prior to its withdrawal just over three months later in December. The large building on the hill seen beyond the loading gauge is West Wycombe House, the ancestral seat of the Dashwood family and home to the notorious 'Hellfire Club'. *RCR7160*

Ref 43. Near Saunderton on 9 April 1958, a 'Westernised' WD No. 90174 from Southall shed plods northwards with a lengthy Class F unfitted freight which looks to be comprised of aging wooden mineral wagons of North Eastern origin. The engine arrived at Southall from Ebbw Junction shed in June 1952 and remained there until withdrawn in October 1962. It received the standard Western Region modifications i.e. the distinctive covered top feed and the sloping 'tunnel' for the fire irons and at the time was one of six of the class allocated at Southall. *RCR11593*

Ref 44. The Up V05 8.55am Birkenhead – Paddington express headed by No. 6025 *King Henry III* speeds through Saunderton station on 1 December 1960. The station, first opened on 1 July 1901, was a latecomer to the Princes Risborough/ Aylesbury extension of the Wycombe Railway and was remodelled for the Joint line and reopened for passengers as from 2 April 1906. The main station building was burnt down in March 1913 by local Suffragettes who may have chosen the location as an easy, but prominent public target. After eleven years at Laira shed, No. 6025 spent the last three years of her career at Old Oak Common shed and was one of the last to be withdrawn in December 1962. *H1922*

Ref 45. Emphasising how lonely life could be even at a main line station, 14XX No. 1473 of Aylesbury shed (a 'sub' of Neasden) drifts into an almost deserted Saunderton station on 1 December 1960 with the 1.52pm for High Wycombe. The train had probably originated from Aylesbury where No. 1473 was based. The 1950s Little Guide series devoted to Buckinghamshire had this to say about the station - *by its name, is calculated to be a snare to the unwary visitor* – a true fact given the village of Saunderton lay over three miles away! No 1473, a regular on these workings since arriving at Aylesbury in October 1953, had not long to work in the area as it was transferred to Gloucester Horton Road shed in January 1961 and withdrawn from there in August 1962. *H1923*

Ref 46-47. A sequence of photographs taken on 14 April 1962 with another Southall WD, this time 90466, with an Up freight in the cutting of the single line 1 in 164 descent from the 83 yard Saunderton Tunnel. Up ahead is the Lee Road bridge where the Up and Down lines resumed company once more on the way to Saunderton station. The divergence of the lines for a distance of approximately 2½ miles allowed Up line trains (particularly heavily loaded coal trains bound for London) to avoid intervening and adverse gradients of 1 in 88 and 1 in 100. The WD was reallocated north five months later and finished its career at Colwick shed, Nottingham, in December 1965. The Vulcan-built engine first appeared in traffic in May 1944 as War Department No. 8661 and was renumbered successively as 78661, LNER 3145, before receiving 63145, its first BR number in June 1948 before renumbered as 90466 from December 1950. Coincidentally, its first allocation from December 1945 as an LNER engine was at Colwick shed so its career could be said to have travelled in full circle!
S1554/S1556.

Ref 48. At Princes Risborough on 18 April 1964, a gaggle of 'spotter oiks' may have 'copped' *Gresley* V2 2-6-2 No. 60963 as it passed with an Up Class C parcels service. Although bereft of a shed plate, records show the engine was based at York at this date and remained there until withdrawn in June 1965. To the left of the train is one of the Marylebone-based Derby 4-car DMU sets (Class 115) which were introduced on the line in January 1961. By the start of the new June 1962 timetable, these units had displaced steam power on all the suburban services to and from Aylesbury, High Wycombe and Princess Risborough and were destined to continue unchallenged in this role for over forty years. *S2642.*

Ref 49. Looking dwarfed by the spacious surroundings of Princes Risborough station, Collett 14XX 0-4-2T No. 1473 leaves platform 3 with an Up service for High Wycombe and possibly the Maidenhead branch. The autotrailer is Diagram A39 No. W220W originally built in 1951 as a Diagram 38 vehicle but rebuilt in February 1952 and named Thrush. Helping to date the photograph, the coach was known to have operated in the London Division until moved to Exeter in mid-1963. In the early 1900s the original station was moved some 100 yards to the south, remodelled and quadrupled to anticipate the 2 April 1906 opening of the Joint line for passenger services. Goods wagons occupy the adjacent platform edge which was not a dedicated bay for any of the branch line services but used as part of the goods yard facility. Beyond this were two private sidings serving Risborough Furniture Ltd. *LS730*

Ref 50. Although in dismal external condition more suited to 'the end of steam era', 4994 Downton Hall looks to be in fine internal fettle as it storms through the southern approaches of Princes Risborough with an Up Class F freight on 1 December 1960. To the left, a 61XX 2-6-2 departs with a Thame – Oxford service. The 'Hall' had been a Didcot engine since February 1953 and would soldier on there until withdrawn in March 1963 – although there is a hint it was stored for a while rather than being condemned outright. At this date, the Western Region suffered a high level of diesel failures resulting in the use of replacement steam power – often with these being resuscitated from scrap lines. After the date of the photograph No. 4994 visited Swindon Works once more prior to being condemned – this being a 'Heavy Intermediate' overhaul and repair undertaken during May and June 1961. Downton Hall is a Grade II Georgian mansion at Stanton Lacy, near Ludlow, Shropshire. *H1901*

Ref 51. The 1950s era, when Marylebone expresses such as the *Master Cutler* saw Neasden and Leicester-based A3 Pacifics using the Joint line, lasted until the summer of 1957 when they were transferred away. Near the end of that era, on 15 June 1957, Leicester-based 60104 Solario hurries through Princes Risborough with a Down express. The engine had the melancholy distinction of being the first of the class to be withdrawn in December 1959 during a visit to Doncaster for repair. The King's Cross-based engine had arrived at the same time as a younger classmate was in for repair (No. 60089 Felstead built in 1928) but because Solario was older (built in 1923), plus considered to be 'too far gone', she was condemned with some of her parts cannibalised to repair Felstead. *H62*

Ref 52. Collett Class '2251' 0-6-0 No. 2270 from Banbury shed (84C) shuffles through the Down loop at Princes Risborough with a Class K local pick-up freight. Helping to date the photograph to the mid-1950s is the first BR 'cycling lion' emblem on the tender plus the relatively early withdrawal date of the engine from Banbury in September 1959. When built in the early 1930s to relieve the earlier 'Dean Goods' 0-6-0s from some of their main line duties, these GWR 'maid of all work' 0-6-0s were something of a sensation with their taper boilers, large cabs with side windows providing extra and much welcome protection from the elements for the crews. Banbury shed had seven or eight of the class in the mid-1950s which were regularly seen on Joint line freight duties. *JH63*

Ref 53. Unlike the Collett 61XX Large Prairie 2-6-2Ts which monopolised the suburban workings out of Paddington until the arrival of the DMUs, their '5101' Class brethren were not generally seen on passenger services much further south than High Wycombe. Demonstrating the point, on 9 July 1960 Banbury's No. 4149 has arrived at Princes Risborough – possibly from Aylesbury - on a very wet evening and will depart with a featherweight 7.25pm service to High Wycombe consisting of one conventional carriage which may be explained by the duty normally being rostered for a single autotrailer service. The engine was a permanent resident at Banbury from February 1950 until condemned in February 1963. *JH1649*

Ref 54. At the north end of Princes Risborough looking south on 9 April 1958, Banbury-based Collett 2-6-2T No. 5152 leaves Princes Risborough for Aylesbury with a service consisting of a single conventional carriage. The panoramic view was taken from the 'North' signal box and includes a veteran Worsdell GER J15 0-6-0 No. 65390 - one of two of the class which transferred to Aylesbury shed in July 1957 to share the Watlington branch goods services after the cessation of passenger services the previous month. No. 65390 had arrived from Cambridge via March and the other, No. 65405, came from Bury St. Edmunds. *RCR11590*

Ref 55-56. A closer look at J15 No. 65390 marshalling stock for the Watlington goods and leaving for the branch on 9 April 1958. The engine was built in October 1890 at Stratford Works and one of a durable and versatile class of 272 dating back to 1883. However, their Watlington exploits were to prove their swansong as both engines were withdrawn later in 1958, 65405 going in mid-August and 65390 in December, their duties taken over by Aylesbury-based LMS Class 2 2-6-2Ts. The impressive 'North' signal box opened for the Joint line in 1904 contained a 126-lever frame measuring 22 yards (the length of a cricket pitch!) and was one of the longest on the GWR. Although it closed in 1991 as a result of extensive resignalling it was saved from demolition - firstly because of its Grade II status and secondly by the efforts of the Chinnor & Princes Risborough Railway Association who aim to restore the building, refit mechanical signalling equipment and re-open it as a working museum. *RCR11588/RCR11591*

Ref 57. On 1 December 1960, Collett 0-6-0PT No. 5420 of Banbury shed leaves Princes Risborough with a single autotrailer service for High Wycombe. The train formed part of a complex roster of duties involving Aylesbury and Banbury-based auto-trains radiating from Princes Risborough and worked by 54XX 0-6-0PTs or 48XX 0-4-2Ts. Typically, the Aylesbury auto-train worked two return trips from Risborough to Banbury whilst the Banbury train worked three with some of the services extended to High Wycombe. During her stay at Banbury shed between January 1958 and September 1961, No. 5420 was regularly seen on these services until moved to the Gloucester area where she was condemned at Barnwood shed in November 1963. *H1915*

Right Ref 58. On 7 October 1961 Collett 'Large Prairie' No. 6123 from Oxford shed percolates in the Risborough Down platform 'West' bay with the usual 2-coach service for the 21 mile Thame branch to Oxford. The train is occupying the bay which was also used by the Watlington passenger services until these ceased on 29 June 1957. Since its appearance in traffic from October 1931, No. 6123 spent all its life within the London Division and was withdrawn from Oxford shed on 5 April 1962. *H3344*

Ref 59. Admired by three lineside spectators, No. 6006 *King George I* of Stafford Road shed hurries the Down 2.10pm Paddington – Wolverhampton express through Princes Risborough on 9 April 1958. Mercifully perhaps for viewing purposes, the usual reporting number boards for this particular service – '916' – have been left off the front of the smokebox. The engine had been allocated to Stafford Road since August 1930 and remained there until 15 February 1962 when it was the first of the class to be withdrawn. It had received a double chimney in June 1956 but its last year in service was interrupted by a succession of lengthy unclassified repairs which may have hastened the decision to condemn early in 1962. Entering Swindon Works on 26 February the engine was in pieces by mid-April. The distinctive, white-painted weatherboarded building behind the spectators is the distinctive, but long-demolished Railway Hotel. RCR11592

Ref 60. Continuing north from Princes Risborough along the main line for two miles, the tiny timber trestle station of Ilmer Halt was reached. This was opened by the GWR on 1 April 1929 with two platforms to serve the local villages of Ilmer and Longwick. Despite its very rural location, four Up and six Down trains still called there in its final months of operation before closure on 5 January 1963. In the last summer of the Master Cutler express operating from Marylebone and with the Chiltern Hills providing the backdrop, Neasden's B1 No. 61187 approaches the station with the Down service on 23 July 1958. The B1 remained on GCR territory until withdrawn from Woodford Halse depot in September 1963. *MM638*

Ref 61. Haddenham Station was conveniently situated on the outskirts of the village and opened in 1906 in conjunction with the Joint line. The station was built with the familiar quadruple track layout and provided with a goods shed, yard and three sidings behind the main station building on the Up side of the line. Beyond Princes Risborough and then Ilmer Halt (opened in 1929) Haddenham was the last station on the Joint line before Ashendon Junction was reached where the line continued north-west on pure GWR metals as the 'Bicester Cut-Off'. On 29 April 1959, the 6.10pm '927' Paddington – Birkenhead service rushes through the station double-headed with a 50XX 'Castle' engine and a 'Hall'- possibly deputising for the more usual 'King' which may have failed. The station closed on 7 January 1963 but was revived, albeit at a new site just over half a mile to the south, as 'Haddenham & Thame Parkway' which opened on 3 October 1987. *MM805*

Ref 62. With the Great Central services from Marylebone operated by the London Midland Region from 1958, the appearance of LMS motive power on main line expresses became common. Typical of these, on 28 April 1959 LMS 'Black 5' No. 44691 of Neasden shed speeds through Haddenham station with the Down 6.18pm Marylebone – Sheffield service. The engine's tenure at Neasden was fairly short, lasting only until July 1960 when a succession of northerly moves took it to Workington where it ended its career in April 1967. *MM806*

Ref 63. Little Kimble station photographed on 11 February 1960. At 2 miles 71 chains 'out' from Princes Risborough on the Aylesbury branch, the station was opened by the GWR on 1 June 1872 and boasted a simple, but attractive gabled brick-built station building together with a platform-width canopy. The station survives as an unstaffed halt, but the station building, now privately-owned, has been sympathetically restored as a domestic property – even the platform canopy survives. The station enjoyed a brief moment of fame in 1998 when, as the nearest station to Chequers, it was used by the Royal Train as a connection to a waiting limousine cavalcade which conveyed the wives of the prominent G8 Summit attendees to their accommodation on the estate. *JH1909*

Ref 64. On 11 February 1960, the Aylesbury-bound autotrailer No. W235W enters the station with Collett 0-6-0PT No. 5420 from Banbury shed suppling the motive power. The trailer was a Diagram A43 63ft vehicle built as recently as 1954 and was also used on the Marlow auto services at this time. It was last recorded in the Yeovil area in early 1965 and was presumably condemned and scrapped there. *JH1913*

Ref 65. In the 1950s, the Aylesbury branch saw around a dozen trains each way with some of these running through to Marylebone and Paddington. On 5 April 1959, Neasden-based Riddles 2-6-4T Class 4 No. 80140 calls at Little Kimble with the 2-coach 8.5am Brackley – Marylebone service. It is likely the train would be strengthened with additional carriage stock at Princes Risborough or High Wycombe. The Class 4 was new to Neasden in July 1956 but would only remain on these services until early 1960 when it was transferred to the Southern Region. With the end of steam on the Region it was withdrawn from Nine Elms shed in July 1967.
MM787

Ref 66. South Aylesbury Halt looking north towards Aylesbury. The station was opened by the GWR on 13 February 1933 as a response to serve local factories and also the growth of the Southcourt housing estate which had begun in the early 1920s. The station was one of many basic unstaffed installations opened during the late 1920s through to the mid-1930s in a bid to stimulate traffic in rural areas without increasing station staff overheads. The station closed on 5 July 1967, although Monks Risborough & Whiteleaf Halt, a similar initiative, opened in November 1929 a short distance to the north of Princes Risborough, was refurbished and remains open doing good business.
AS K85/3

Ref 67. At Aylesbury, Slough-based Large Prairie No. 6167 has arrived at platform 4 with the 3.6pm service from Maidenhead on 4 April 1959. The busy-looking Aylesbury shed seen to the right was a sub-shed of Slough and until 1948 had a permanent allocation of up to three outstationed 61XX 2-6-2Ts allocated for the High Wycombe-Maidenhead- Slough- Paddington services and these continued to work through from Slough after the transfer of the shed as a 'sub' to Neasden. No. 6167 was a long-term Slough resident and a familiar sight at Aylesbury until June 1964 when it moved to Southall. A late overhaul at Swindon during May 1963 enabled it to survive almost to the end of GWR steam in October 1965.
MM785

Ref 68. A nicely cleaned Collett 14XX 0-4-2T No. 1473 is seen again – this time on 23 February 1957 with an arrival at Aylesbury with the 11.13am from Princes Risborough. The '34E' shed plate recording its base as being Neasden's outpost at Aylesbury looks a little odd worn by a GWR engine, but is an interesting, if arcane, item of proof indicating the 'joint' nature of Aylesbury's past railway history. *LRF2634*

Ref 69. A closer look at Aylesbury shed on 11 February 1960. The structure existed from late 1863 in conjunction with the arrival of the Wycombe Railway, firstly as a single-road accommodation and then enlarged to 2 roads by the GWR in the 1870s. By 1908 and now jointly owned by the GWR, GCR and the Metropolitan, it was upgraded and improved again with a northlight building overlaid on the footprint of the first structure. Until 1948 it was a sub-shed of Slough, but after 1948 was 'subbed' to Neasden shed. In 1954 its allocation was an eclectic mix of one GWR 14XX 0-4-2T and/or a 54XX 0-6-0PT, one LMS Class 4 2-6-4T, one LNER L1 2-6-4T, two LNER N5 0-6-2Ts and two BR Standard Class 2 2-6-0s. The shed was closed along with its parent in June 1962 but continued to service visiting engines into 1963 with some of these arriving from Cricklewood shed which had assumed responsibility for the remaining Neasden duties. No. 5420 with auto trailer lurks further along platform 4 with an auto service to Princes Risborough.
JH1914

Ref 70. With Aylesbury shed in such close proximity to the station there was no need for 'spotters' to 'bunk' it as everything was fully on view from platform 4. The shed's modest facilities, although updated during the first decade of the 20th Century, in part relied on the modification of what was already there. The manual coal stage was a case in point having been adapted from the ribs of the original water tower. A small turntable (possibly 24ft?) which had existed at the front of the building on the engine road nearest the water tower was recorded as 'disused' by 1924 but not removed until after 1931. W235W waits to return to Princes Risborough on 11 February 1960 hauled by Collett 0-6-0PT No. 5420.
JH1903

Ref 70A. The same train seen from its business end featuring No. 5420 of Banbury shed. *H1907*

Ref 71. At Aylesbury on 23 February 1957, Riddles Class 4 2-6-4T No. 80139 shunts empty Metropolitan Railway carriage stock at platform 3. The engine is barely eight months old and was delivered new to Neasden from Brighton Works on 26 June 1956 – one of a batch of eight of the class (Nos. 80137 – 44) to arrive there from May to September that year. No. 80139 remained at Neasden until early January 1960 when, along with its seven other classmates, it was transferred to the Southern Region. It subsequently moved between Brighton, Redhill and Eastleigh sheds and survived until the end of the Region's steam on 9 July 1967.
LRF2632

Ref 72. At Aylesbury on 11 February 1960, Neasden's smart B1 4-6-0 No 61078 with Leicester's scruffy BR Class 5 No. 73010 double head a modestly loaded Up service to Marylebone. The lightness of the train possibly suggests the B1 is working forward with the train to save a light engine path to its destination. Along with seven other Leicester-based BR Class 5s No. 73010 would become a Neasden engine the following June and would eventually finish at Patricroft shed where it was withdrawn in June 1968. The B1 would remain active on GCR metals until withdrawn from Woodford Halse shed in October 1962.
JH1906

Ref 73. Aylesbury had the attraction of the GCR main line Master Cutler and South Yorkshireman expresses until these were taken off the route in 1958 and 1960, respectively. Sometime in the summer of 1957, Leicester-based A3 4-6-2 No. 60102 *Sir Frederick Banbury* has arrived at its last stop before Marylebone with the Up South Yorkshireman. Of the eleven or so A3s based at Leicester and Neasden since c.1949 for the GCR services on the main line and the 'Joint', it was said that No. 60102 was the pick of the bunch but despite this was one of the six which were condemned in 1961 with No. 60102 going from King's Cross in November. *NS205632*

Ref 74. Although 'pegged' for departure, B1 4-6-0 No. 61274 of Bradford Low Moor shed may be about to take on water at the north end of Aylesbury's platform 3 on 2 July 1960. Mindful of public sensitivities, the sign attached to the water column for the benefit of enginemen reads: 'SMOKE NUISANCE. WHILE ENGINES STAND AT THIS WATER CRANE THEY MUST NOT EMIT EXCESSIVE SMOKE.' The footbridge in front of the engine did not connect with the station but accessed the town to an area on the south side of line known as 'California'. The platform 4 line to the left ran back and branched off to access the engine shed. *H1572*

Ref 75. On Saturday 14 May 1960, Collett Large Prairie 2-6-2T No. 6132 of Old Oak Common shed has arrived at the west end of Thame station with the Down 11.40am from Princes Risborough and is taking water prior to running round the train for the return Up 12.10am departure for Paddington. Fireman D. Perry is in charge of the leather 'bag' from the water column. *JH1247*

Ref 76. No. 6132 has now attached itself to the rear of the 11.40am arrival and prepares to move the stock over ready for the 12.10am departure. A gaggle of small boys at a loose end look on from the Up platform hoping for a footplate visit – which a few minutes later they got! Thame was the most important station on the line, was fully equipped with goods and passenger facilities and most associated with its distinctive 90ft long all-timber train shed seen in the background. This structure was part of the original 1862 terminus of the line prior to its extension to Oxford when the train shed was enlarged to cover two platforms. The building was demolished soon after the passenger services ceased in January 1963 and the site is now part of an industrial estate and housing development.
JH1249

Ref 77. At Thame looking east towards the goods yard on the evening of 9 July 1960, Collett '5101' Class Large Prairie No. 4125 of Oxford shed enters with a service from Princes Risborough. At much the same time the branch was under a pre-Beeching scrutiny by Western Region area management for possible closure to passengers (apart from workers' trains from Oxford to Cowley at the western end of the line) and the withdrawal of some freight services. This move was finally enacted for passengers as from 7 January 1963 and through freight services on the line were gradually pinched out until by 1 May 1967 only the western stub was left at Littlemore (for oil traffic), as far as Cowley (for car traffic) and an eastern stub as far as Thame for a large oil depot. The latter traffic ceased as from October 1991 leaving only the section of the line from 'Thame Junction' into Princes Risborough's platform 4 which is now used by the Chinnor & Princes Risborough Railway.
JH1645

Ref 78. Watched by the Thame signalman with the single line token and carrier, the crew of Oxford's '5101' Class Large Prairie No. 4148 prepare to take on water at the east end of Thame station prior to leaving with a service for Princes Risborough on 9 July 1960. The very last passenger train on the branch was strengthened to five carriages instead of the normal two and left Oxford for Princes Risborough at 5.50pm hauled by Oxford's 61XX No. 6111. The return from Risborough to Oxford left at 7.20pm. *H1644*

Ref 79. At 2 miles 75 chains 'out' from Princes Risborough, Wainhill Crossing Halt on the Watlington branch was a tiny rail-level platform opened by the GWR on 1 August 1925 as part of their efforts to drum up extra trade in rural areas. Wainhill was so remote that the Thame Gazette was moved to comment somewhat tartly that 'It will serve the hills chiefly'. Nevertheless, the station remained open for business until the passenger service ceased in 1957. In this photograph the guard has set down the auto-trailer steps to platform level and is ready to assist any ascending or descending passenger. The set of wooden steps seen outside the bike shed doubled as spare boarding steps when a conventional carriage was in use and also as 'assists' for staff to reach up to hook the platform lamps onto the platform posts. *H65*

Ref 80. The brick and flint rural charm of Chinnor Station as seen on 23 September 1951. The station was 3 miles 57 chains from Princes Risborough and built in a mid-Victorian gothic pavilion style that was also used at Aston Rowant and Watlington. Mr Wilkinson of Lucas & Wilkinson, the Westminster civil engineering firm which constructed the line, may have been responsible for the design as similar railway projects he was involved with in other parts of the country also produced the same style of building. Although the station building was demolished after the closure of the line, it has been faithfully rebuilt in its original style and on the same site by the Chinnor & Princes Risborough Railway Association. *RCR3455*

Ref 81. A general view of Watlington goods yard looking south-west towards the station on 23 February 1957 with Slough-based 0-6-0PT No. 5766 in charge of the auto train. The yard, with its parked wagons on the 'back road' on the right, gives a deceptively busy appearance but in truth, like the passenger numbers, traffic had been in decline for years. The diminutive Watlington signal box seen between the goods shed and the train once controlled the modest signalling arrangements until these were dispensed with c.1928 with the branch continuing as a 'one engine in steam' operation with the single line train staff. *LRF2639*

Ref 82. One of the other regular Slough-based Collett 0-6-0PTs used on the branch, No. 3697, is seen at Watlington on 15 June 1957 preparing to run round the auto trailer to take on water for the trip back to Princes Risborough. The corrugated structure on the right was a survivor from W&PRR days erected as protection for standby carriages and occasionally in later years for cleaning the branch auto trailer. Miraculously, the structure, although dilapidated, still survives to this day. Beyond the train and opposite the water tank on the right was the site of the wooden engine shed which, after it was burnt down in 1906 and never replaced, still continued to be used as a coaling and stabling point. *JH66*

Left, Ref 83. No. 3697 takes on water at Watlington before returning with the auto train for the 8 mile 66 chain run to Princes Risborough. The Slough-based engines returned to their parent shed at the end of the working week for a boiler washout and any other repairs needed. No. 3697 remained at Slough until transferred to Didcot in March 1962 where it was condemned eight weeks later. The GWR pillar water tank was recovered from Taunton and re-erected at Watlington in August 1919 as a replacement for the original wooden structure. *JH68*

Right, Ref 84. Last rites for the passenger service on Saturday 29 June 1957 as Collett 0-6-0PT No. 4650 from Slough shed officiates. On the very last train from Princes Risborough, the stock was strengthened with an extra carriage to pack in almost 200 passengers bidding farewell to the branch. The line stayed open for residual goods traffic until 2 January 1961 but then cut back to Chinnor for local traffic until October 1966 after which it was used solely for the Chinnor Cement Works. This traffic lasted until December 1989 when the section was closed. Fortunately, this final part of the line survives as the Chinnor and Princes Risborough Railway Association. *LN1232*

Ref 85. On 27 June 1957, two days before closure to passengers, Watlington Station and goods shed slumber in the late afternoon sunshine. Just visible is a pannier tank ready for probably the last departure of the day at around 7.15pm. The GWR 'Toad' brake van parked at the end of the loading dock had been used as a replacement mess room since 1951 after its predecessor, a grounded horse-box, was destroyed by fire. Regrettably, the station building was left to deteriorate and what little remains now is heavily overgrown and on private property.
AEB2195A